JOHN WINTERS

The Delta Force

Copyright © John Winters, 2018

All rights reserved. No part of this publication may be reproduced, stored or transmitted in any form or by any means, electronic, mechanical, photocopying, recording, scanning, or otherwise without written permission from the publisher. It is illegal to copy this book, post it to a website, or distribute it by any other means without permission.

John Winters has no responsibility for the persistence or accuracy of URLs for external or third-party Internet Websites referred to in this publication and does not guarantee that any content on such Websites is, or will remain, accurate or appropriate.

First edition

This book was professionally typeset on Reedsy.
Find out more at reedsy.com

Contents

Introduction	iv
The World of Delta Force	1
Delta Force Exists, Delta Force Doesn't Exist?	7
Delta Force Missions: Declassified	12
Organization, Structure, Training and Recruitment	21
Delta Force Origins	32
The Arsenal	37
At the End Of the Day	41
Why DELTA Operators Are Unique	48
PART 2 - The Difference Between Delta, SEAL Team SIX and...	57
GREEN BERETS	63
NAVY SEALS	93
SEAL Team Six	124
Special Air Service	127
Conclusion	155

Introduction

Special Forces Units are usually secretive in most aspects of their activities. The Delta Force takes this secrecy to a whole new level.

Not much is known about this Elite Unit. Many have heard stories about the unit and about the brave men that serve in it's ranks, but the story of Delta Force remains shrouded in secrecy.

Delta Force is a unit that "unofficially" exists inside the US Army. Only the best of the best makes it into the ranks of this unit. Their missions are mostly never reported or talked about. They operate in the shadows. Many of their successes get credited to other more high profile units.

In this book, I will tell the story of arguably the best Special Forces Unit in the World. I will share with you what is known about this elite Unit.

I hope you enjoy this book and thank you for downloading.

1

The World of Delta Force

Take the time to consider a special, powerful operations force within the United States military that's fully trained and prepared in the highest possible levels. Such force could only be well funded, and armed with today's cutting edge weaponry. And they only answer to one man.

But how can this highly-trained group, to the point of wearing the "mercenaries" status wherever they go, be reeled in and thrust into the limelight if the U.S. government would not even confirm its existence?

Better known as the 1st Special Forces Operational Detachment – Delta, Delta Force is a component of the U.S. Army within the Joint Special Operations Command (JSOC). The Department of Defense (DoD) listed the group as a Combat Applications Group (CAG) back then, though some have claimed the group was redesigned and reintroduced as the Army Compartmented Elements (ACE).

While the United States Army Special Operations Command (USASOC) administratively backs the 1st SFOD-D, the group falls in line with the Joint Special Operations Command (JSOC). The Delta Force, together with the Naval Special Warfare Development Group (its Navy counterpart), are highly regarded as the main counter-terrorism units of the U.S. military.

Aside from counter-terrorism, the Delta Force is also tasked to take direct action and handle national intervention operations, though the group is extremely versatile and capable of conducting almost any type of mission. These include, but are not limited to raids and hostage rescues.

While the group often fills up its ranks from Army Special Forces (Green Berets) and shares headquarters with them in Fort Bragg, N.C., it is anything but a conventional Army Special Forces Unit. The Delta Force is a complete unit unto itself; it is composed of soldiers coming from all military branches.

The highly secretive Special Activities Division (SAD) of the Central Intelligence Agency (CIA), together with the Special Operations Group (SOG) often recruits Delta Force operators – they even work with Delta Force operators from time to time on various missions.

Instead of being called soldiers, members of the Delta Force are addressed as operators. They are known to shun various traditional philosophies revolving around military life, which is most evident in their practice of wearing civilian clothes. And for a good reason – such approach serves their purpose very well.

Always on the ready, they can work for anyone who needs their special skills: the Army, CIA, and even the FBI. In his controversial book "Blackhawk Down," author Mark Bowden interviewed many Delta Force operators, all of them claiming they are "professional soldiers who simply hate the Army."

THE DELTA FORCE

2

Delta Force Exists, Delta Force Doesn't Exist?

It must be understood that both the U.S. government and military do not officially acknowledge the group's existence. To this day, almost everything we know about the most elite tactical group in the American military is not supported by official government reports.

It is only recently that certain references made by the government regarding the groups' existence and operations were allowed to roam freely on air. Such references were heard during congressional hearings and especially biographies of top-ranking military leaders.

The thing is keeping a force so deadly efficient with a stuff-for-legend reputation under wraps is next to impossible. Ever since its inception to the world of special operations back in 1977, stories and adventures of the group's exploits have surfaced out bit by bit. And as time goes by, we have painted a clearer picture of the unit and what it does.

The group came under the microscope back in 1993 during a failed operation to interdict a Somali warlord. Delta Force operators were among those who fought and died during that fateful event. The group was also thrust into the limelight in 1983 during Operation Urgent Fury. Delta Force conducted 2 missions in Grenada – one successful and one failed. Both missions then became common knowledge to the special operations community.

Delta has been repeatedly criticized for taking on missions that goes beyond regular laws that governed the military. Such revelations had many worried that the unit carries more power than perceived and less accountability as compared to other military organizations operating in the democratic world.

According to some press reports, the funding of Delta comes from secret government accounts free from public scrutiny. The US government has not commented on these press speculations. Many believe this serves them better in their task to help maintain the United States' role as a superpower policing the world. Their capabilities present America with more flexibility and more room to maneuver.

The reality is that in today's political environment and the growing threat of terrorism means that Delta is even more needed than ever before.

DELTA FORCE EXISTS, DELTA FORCE DOESN'T EXIST?

3

Delta Force Missions: Declassified

Delta Force's first ever mission came shortly after it was formed – guarding the Puerto Rico Pan-American Games back in 1979. While the detailed mission went smoothly, their next mission was considered a failure.

Operation Eagle Claw

Shortly after the Delta Force unit was created, 53 American citizens and diplomats were taken hostage inside the U.S. Embassy in Iran on November 4, 1979. The unit was ordered to mount a covert operation to enter the country and recover the hostages by force on the 24th and 25th of April in 1980. The operation was aborted because of aviation failures. Later in the review commission, it was found out that the failure was due to a range of problems that plagued the operation.

Among such problems was the failure to brief the aviation part of the operation of the weather on time and take the appropriate steps to deal with the situation. Another pressing issue that had to be addressed was "command-and-control" between the multi-service component commanders, which resulted in a helicopter and ground refueling aircraft collision. There were also mechanical problems that finally reduced what available helicopters the operation had to put into play before the whole group could leave for the operation.

The U.S. government quickly realized that more changes and improvements needed to be made after the failed operation. This resulted in the creation of the "Night Stalkers," officially known as the 160th Special Operations Aviation Regiment. The unit was made exclusively for special operations needing aviation support.Specialized air support has become the norm in all special operations around the world.

The unit carried out one memorable textbook operation back in the 80s at least. And this was based on what Delta Force was made to do – rescue hostages in tight spaces in the most efficient way possible. Operators(Operators is the term used for special forces soldiers) gained access of a hijacked Indonesian plane, rescued the hostages and killed all four hijackers on the plane.

This was not the last time Delta Force was called on to handle airline hostage situations, though they were barred by local authorities from executing rescue operations on hijacked airliners in Kuwait and other countries.

After being called into action, Delta Force would arrive into the scene battle-ready, only to find out that they were not wanted and that the political role players did not create the correct environment to work in. And this would eventually become a pattern for the unit. A good example would be in the early 80s when Delta Force was tasked to rescue American POWs in Vietnam. Each of the planned missions got canceled.

Operation Urgent Fury

This was the Grenada prisoner rescue operation by Delta Force operators in Richmond Hill prison. It was also among the missions the unit overtly executed alongside the U.S. military's major invasions.

In this operation, the Delta operators were put in an extremely hostile environment and was put under extremely heavy crossfire by the Grenada Military.Several of the pilots flying the Delta Operators to their destination aborted the mission without any orders to do so.Delta operators were shocked with the unprofessional actions of some pilots and made an official complaint.

Operation Just Cause

Back in 1989, the operation was geared towards the Panama invasion with the aim of capturing President Noriega and at the same time protecting 35,000 Americans in Panama at that time.

The Gulf War

Iraq had just invaded Kuwait, and with Delta Force at the tip of the spear, the US-led alliance defeated Saddam Hussein's army, pushing them back to Iraq.

This was perhaps Delta Force's most widely known operation. Dubbed as the "Great Scud Hunt," Delta Force operators and SAS operators, were tasked to take part in Operation Desert Storm. Their mission was simple, infiltrate Iraqi territory, locate hidden Scud missiles and call in an airstrike.While doing that, they were also tasked with disrupting the enemy.

The operators also served as General Norman Schwarzkopf's bodyguard during this time. And acting as bodyguards for high-profile individuals is a role the unit continues to perform these days. This is evident in photos purporting Delta Force operators guarding President Hamid Karzai of Afghanistan.

Sometimes Delta operators look like civilian bodyguards because they do not wear normal US army uniforms.Most of the time Delta Operators wear civilian clothing and have beards.This helps them blend in with society.

Operation Gothic Serpent

This operation was part of the Mogadishu(Somalia) Battle in 1993. U.S. helicopters were being shot down from the sky with RPGs. Delta operators were awarded the Congressional Medal of Honor due to their valiant efforts that day.

The events that played out in Mogadishu was depicted in the 2001 movie Black Hawk Down.The movie was based on a book by Mark Bowden about the events in Mogadishu in 1993.

The objective of this mission was to capture the warlord leader Aidid. As part of the main objective, they were sent to arrest 2 of Aidid's main officers. These events led to what was shown in the movie Black Hawk Down. If you saw the movie, then you know what happened. The mission did not go according to plan, and a small group of Delta operators and Rangers were killed in action. Many Somalian fighters were killed.

This battle of Mogadishu led to the withdrawal of US troops from Somalia. The situation was so lawless and dangerous in Somalia that shortly after the UN(United Nations) also withdrew from Somalia.

The War in Afghanistan

Just a month after the 9/11 attacks on the American mainland, Delta Force, Navy SEALS and the British SAS aided the global effort in defeating the Taliban and dismantling them from where they stood in Afghanistan afterward.These units conducted a wide range of operations, one of these operations was Operation Tora Bora.

The Battle of Tora Bora

This was an enormous joint engagement to capture or kill Osama Bin Laden.The US intelligence community believed that Bin Laden was hiding in the Tora Bora mountains.

The US and allied forces destroyed most of the Taliban and Al-Qaeda positions but failed to capture Bin Ladin, who escaped into Pakistan, where he stayed for almost a decade.

The role of the Delta Force in Afghanistan continues today. Delta Force will probably be involved in Afghanistan for many years to come.At the moment not much in known about details of their current mission in Afghanistan, it remains classified

Operation Iraqi Freedom 2003

Delta operators were involved in a wide range of operations in Iraq; the most famous of these was Operation Red Dawn.

Operation Red Dawn 2003

The operation was all about the effort to locate and capture Saddam Hussein.Operation Red Dawn was initiated after gaining credible intelligence identifying two likely locations of Saddam Hussein.

Operation Red Dawn was a massive operation;it consisted of 600 soldiers(infantry, cavalry) including a group of Delta operators. Delta was to lead the operation supported by a large group of conventional forces. Their mission instructions were simple; they were to capture or kill Sadam Hussein.

After a lengthy search, they were successful. Hussein was found hiding in the bottom of a hole.

ISIS

According to recent press reports, the Delta Force and British Special Forces are combining to deal with the current situation in Iraq and Syria. The current situation is that a terrorist group has taken control of large parts of Iraq. According to reports, Delta and SAS operators have been tasked to conduct missions in the area to disrupt the current situation.

Other Operations

And then there were all those countless hostage rescues all over the world where Delta Force operators actively took part in the operations.

The Delta Force is constantly called to deal with dangerous situations across the globe. The growing threat of terrorism means that Delta will be called upon to deal with many more operations.

Most of Delta operations will be classified and not mentioned in the news.

4

Organization, Structure, Training and Recruitment

As already mentioned, the unit belongs to the USASOC, though operational control is given to JSOC. Command of Delta Force is a Colonel's billet. All data about the unit is classified; any detail regarding specific missions are not made available to the public. We can be content, however, on some sources (including "Inside Delta Force",2003, by Sergeant Major Eric L. Haney, retired) that suggested unit strength to be anywhere from 800 to 1,000 personnel.

Detachment Designations

The structure of Delta Force is very similar to that of the British 22 SAS. In the book "Not a Good Day to Die: The Untold Story of Operation Anaconda(Sean Naylor,2006)," unit strength was described to having nearly 1,000 soldiers. Army Times writer Sean Naylor recorded that approximately a quarter of the unit were operators constantly trained to conduct recon and direct action missions. These operators were designated to 3 main operational squadrons: A, B, and C squadrons respectively.

These squadron formations were based on the SAS "Sabre Squadron" organization, where every squadron would contain about 75 to 85 operators. Each squadron would also be broken down into three troop types: two assault/direct action troops and one sniper/recon troop. All involved could flexibly operate groups or teams having only up to 6 men.

Recruits are chosen based on their special skills – one of them is exceptional marksmanship. It has been reputed that the recruits remarkably show 90% accuracy when shooting at a thousand yards and 100% accuracy from six hundred yards. A forty-mile hike endurance test was also implemented to single out the more capable who stood out from among those who manage to remain in the training. The approach was adopted from SAS philosophies.

Delta Force also holds recruitment drives nationwide for several months, which then culminate into two distinct selection processes, the first one in spring, and the other during fall. During these month-long selection processes, recruits who survive would move to the tougher part of the training process, which would last for 6 months.

THE DELTA FORCE

One of the most detailed books on the Delta Force is a book by Eric Haney(2003).(Highly recommended book)In the book, he describes the initial selection process.The selection process is modeled on the selection process of the British SAS.Like the SAS, the selection begins with standard tests like push-ups, sit-ups, pull-ups and a 2-mile run.This is followed up by a crawl and 100-meter swimming exercise while fully dressed and wearing combat boots.

Next is the old-school SAS style marches.The first one is an 18-mile navigation march at night.The soldiers do this night march with a 40-pound backpack.The weight of the backpack and the course distance gets increased with every march.The last march takes place in rough terrain and covers a distance of 40 miles with a 45-pound backpack.The time limit for the last march is unknown for the recruits.At this stage of selection, the bodies and minds of recruits have already been tested to the extreme.These physical tests are followed up by a wide range of psychological tests that takes the candidates to their mental limits. If the recruits pass this initial selection process, they move on to an intense 6-month training course.(Inside Delta Force, Eric Haney,2003)

Operator Training Course (OTC)

The OTC course constantly improves the skills being taught broadly these days. It generally includes the following:

- Marksmanship
- Demolitions and Breaching
- Combined Skills
- Trade Craft
- Executive Protection

Trainees utilize several training facilities for demolition and marksmanship training about counter-terrorist and hostage rescue simulations, including other settings as well.

They then learn how to set up effective sniper positions on urban establishments. They also learn how to set a TOC (tactical operations center) properly and communicate efficiently.

Delta Force may have specialized sniper troops, but everyone has to progress through this training. Along the way, real operators would train with them and exercises would then use live ammunition. This is to test the students and build trust among each other. Operators also learn espionage-related skills like dead drops and surveillance. Delta Force training is topped by a culmination exercise.

There are also support groups that aid Delta Force's 3 combat squadrons during operations: the aviation platoon, support and signal squadron, and their intelligence gathering outfit dubbed, "the funny platoon." Supposedly, this particular sub-unit includes women.

The main combat groups are broken down into smaller units (troops) each. They specialize in either ground, airborne, and even water insertion just like in the tactical insertion system of the Green Berets.

Coming from various military backgrounds, the recruits have already been trained to eliminate hostile targets. As operators of Delta Force, however, they become efficient, trained killers. And with their counter-terrorist tags, the operators are thoroughly trained in hostage rescues in tight spaces. Hostage takers are taken out after securing their objectives (rescuing hostages). Beckwith implemented the two-tap shot method when dealing with hostiles; each terrorist must be dealt with two shots.

Operators are instructed not to spare hostiles who would later come back and fight another day. This is in stark contrast to various TV and movie representations of the unit.

ORGANIZATION, STRUCTURE, TRAINING AND RECRUITMENT

5

Delta Force Origins

As the Navy's Special Warfare Development Group (DEVGRU-SEAL TEAM SIX), Delta Force could readily deploy anywhere needed. Unlike

SEAL TEAM SIX however, the unit does not officially exist.

Even if Delta is mainly a tier-one counter-terrorism unit, directed to either capture or kill high-value targets (HVU) specifically or destroy terrorist cells, the unit remains quite flexible to adapt to most situations. You can also count on them to engage in various direct action missions, or work covertly to provide high-ranking protective services for America's senior leaders.

When compared to America's military history, Delta Force is relatively young. It all started back in 1977 with Vietnam War veteran Colonel Beckwith, its first ever commander. Delta came out as both a necessity and solution to the increasingly growing threats of terrorism all over the world.

The 70's saw the scary outbreak of extremism. Groups like the Palestinian Liberation Organization and Germany's Red Army Faction introduced the world to "hijacking" and "terrorism." Colonel Beckwith realized the need for a top-of-the-line small, yet highly-skilled tactical team fully capable of responding to such threats with quick and deadly force.He realized the need for such a unit after having worked with the famed British Special Air Service (SAS) back in the early 70's.

Colonel Beckwith was tasked with forming a new and special unit with members coming from various existing Special Forces groups in the U.S. military. And the mission types they had been involved with over time were classified though some have been notably declassified and referenced in both media reports and some books authored by Delta operators.

Colonel Beckwith had a documented stint as an exchange officer with the 22 SAS Regiment(Special Air Service) during the Malayan Emergency. The SAS is the grandfather of modern Special Forces units and an elite United Kingdom Special Forces unit. They were the pioneers of modern special warfare.

The experience with the SAS made a profound impression on Colonel Beckwith. The SAS was operating in the shadows in the 1950s and 1960s, and the methods and structure of the SAS were unknown and unique. The SAS was operating in small groups behind enemy lines using commando techniques to disrupt and destroy the enemy. These SAS troopers were highly trained men, with extreme fitness levels and extraordinary individual skills.

He was impressed with how these SAS troopers could operate on an elite level with limited supplies and equipment. These SAS Operators were operating on a different level than other "Special Forces Units" in the world.

Upon his return, Colonel Beckwith detailed a report highlighting the vulnerability of the U.S. Army without an SAS-type unit. Existing Special Forces within the army at that time focused only on unconventional warfare.

Beckwith pointed out the need to evolve from exclusively "being teachers" to "being doers" as well. He painted a very clear picture of highly adaptable, yet completely autonomous units armed with a very wide array of special skills for both counter terrorism and direct missions. He was given the opportunity to brief government and military figures who, back then, were resisting the idea of creating a whole new unit outside of the existing Special Forces (Green Berets).

When the threat of terrorism sprang out from just about anywhere around the world in the mid 70's, the Pentagon finally gave Colonel Beckwith the go signal to form such special unit. He had estimated that getting a new unit to be mission-ready would take 24 months. The estimate came about from an earlier conversation with Brigadier John Watts about his SAS experience in 1976. Watts emphasized that Beckwith would need 18 months to build an efficient squadron though he insisted that Beckwith would be better off with a whole 24 months just to get the unit mission ready.(Beckwith,2013,Delta Force: A Memoir by the Founder of the U.S. Military's Most Secretive Special-Operations Unit)

The Arsenal

Delta Force operators become the best at what they do inside the "House of Horrors." This training facility is where they work tirelessly to hone their skills. It is specially designed to include trains, buses, and passenger airplanes to simulate various environments where they develop and test their hostage-rescue operational skills. Such setup is

The unit is believed to rely much on sub-machine guns (specifically the MP5 and M4 light weapon variants) from German weapons manufacturer, Heckler and Koch. They also prize the 7.62mm PSG1 sniper rifle for various recon missions. Apart from the H&K sniper rifle, Delta Force operators were also known to utilize the M82A1 .50-cal sniper rifle of the American manufacturer Browning for much longer targets (at 1,750 yards).

Many insiders within the military community believed that Delta Force is working directly with H&K to come up with a new 416 Carbine assault rifle model that utilizes 5.56mm rounds efficiently. Military experts consider it a suitable replacement for the standard M4. Both powerful sniper rifles and high-performance sub-machine guns alone are never enough to successfully complete most Delta Force missions.

Aside from the extensive training and top-of-the-class weaponry, the unit also relies heavily on air support. This is where operators require their squadron's aviation platoon to complete given missions. The aviation platoon is composed of various aircraft outfitted with civilian-class registration numbers to look just like civilian helicopters.

During situations where U.S. military, government, or specific federal agencies must not get involved officially, the aviation platoon of the unit (serving as civilian aircraft) would deliver and extract battle squadrons, as operators are required to land into the battlefield using civilian clothing. Such flexibility makes Delta a great asset for the US government because officially they do not exist.

In extreme cases, the unit would call upon the "Night Stalkers." They are known officially as a group of highly trained pilots from S.O.A.R. (160th Special Operations Aviation Regiment). They could fly the "Little Bird" and Black Hawk helicopters with extreme efficiency near ground level to avoid radar detection, thus delivering Delta Force operators to the insertion areas successfully. These battle-hardened Night Stalkers utilize advanced night vision technology, as they frequent flying away without lights into the black night with their black helicopters to conceal the insertion of operators in the battlefield and their flight paths as well. They take pride on their ability to get the operators to various destinations all within the +/- 30 seconds required time-frame.

7

At the End Of the Day

Delta Force operators are selected for very specific traits, be it their language skills, their extreme physical endurance, or that special ability to shoot targets half a mile away. They are usually chosen for their lack of showy machismo, which serves them well, given their knack to blend in with civilian life.

We can be certain they are extremely low-key; you could even mistake them for a normal guy next door.Most of the time Delta operators do not wear uniforms, and they are not "officially" members of Delta.They tend to be laid-back, not showy in any way, and slow to anger.Delta Operators have very high levels of self-control.

Psychological strength and mind control in any situation is what make Delta Force operators unique.They are selected and trained firstly on their psychological strengths.These strengths are then turned into assets for the operators.They learn to overcome any psychological barrier that they get confronted with.Like the SAS, Delta knows that the key to becoming a successful operator is mastering your mind and controlling your emotions.

AT THE END OF THE DAY

For one, it's quite difficult to become the best in any given occupation and at the same time sworn to secrecy. Once a soldier becomes a Delta Force operator, he has to dress up as a civilian (grow civilian hair and beard as well) and blend in well with them. Operators live private, secret lives and never tell anyone what they do for a living.

And they train hard on a consistent basis as well. They're ascetics; part of their overall discipline is conditioning themselves digging holes and living inside them for any given time, or being dropped in the middle of nowhere and having to find (or fight) their way out.

Delta Force operators are extremely professional and expect only the highest standards from themselves and fellow operators.Units that work with Delta are always impressed with their skill levels and professional conduct in extreme situations.

Military insiders like to point out that the unit is a haven for good soldiers who hate army life. Delta Force operators are usually older than regular soldiers. They love what they are doing in the unit and simply hate life under the chain of command. Operators call one another by their nicknames; they do not recognize rank. Some of the most respected operators are usually noncoms, or sergeants.

AT THE END OF THE DAY

8

Why DELTA Operators Are Unique

(1)Delta Operators are the ultimate soldiers

Delta Operators are individually capable of executing almost any type of operation.The US Government invests millions of dollars in each operator, making sure they are the finest soldiers on the planet.They learn all traditional and unconventional soldering skills.Physically they have fitness levels of Olympic endurance athletes and have extreme mental toughness.On top of that they get trained by the CIA and FBI to operate within cities.They are capable of speaking more than one language, are experts in mixed martial arts and are highly skilled in close protection of VIP's.They are as close as you get to the fictional characters of James Bond and Jason Bourne.

(2)Delta Force operators will be tasked to maintain a presence in cities that the US President visits.

They will be the insurance policy if something goes wrong, and the secret service can't handle the situation in extreme circumstances.Delta is capable of dealing with most situations with just a small group of operators.

(3)Delta prefers to stay in the shadows; they don't like to be in the spotlight

The Navy Seals get a lot of media attention for high-profile missions, but Delta prefer to stay out of the Hollywood story lines.Delta sees silence and anonymity as power and a tool they use to create uncertainty about their existence.When massive media attention gets put on other Special Forces units, Delta can operate in the background and get things dome while no-one is watching.Many successful Delta missions get credited to other Special Forces Units, conventional units or does not get mentioned in the press.People sometimes forget that officially "Delta does not exist."

(4)The Intelligence levels of potential Delta members are very important

Delta needs soldiers that can think on their feet.They need someone that can act independently, assess the situation and then take action.Delta operators get placed in high-pressure situations that could potentially create international incidents.Therefore, Delta operators need to be able to be independent,intelligent and use their intellect to make critical decisions with limited time ,in high-pressure situations.

(5)Delta Force Operators are the best of the best.

Delta select their members from mostly other Special Forces Groups like the Army Rangers and the Special Forces(Green Berets).Up to 75% of Delta, Operators comes from the 75th Ranger Regiment.The rest are from the Green Berets and other combat units within the US Miltary. Delta also recruits from the US Marine Corps.

(6)Delta operators must have good social skills and be good at communication in any situation

Operators could be placed in many unusual scenarios and then have to blend into the situation without flinching.If you hesitate and act out of place in a real operation, you could pay with your life.For example, a Delta operator could be scuba diving into a location and be dining at a formal event 30 minutes later, and he has to be able to make the social transition effortlessly.

(7) Delta Force is probably the most adaptable Special Forces Unit in the world.

Delta Force is adaptable and completely self-sufficient teams. Delta can operate in almost any conceivable environment. They are comfortable on sea, land, and air. The jungle, desert, and the Arctic are all environments that Delta can comfortably operate in and be successful. They can blend into city environments and act next to civilian agencies and be as comfortable as in any other environment.

(8) Delta members do not wear uniforms.

Delta does not wear conventional uniforms most of the time and mostly look like civilians. Many operators have beards and longer hair. This is one of the ways Delta stays in the shadows.

(9)The Brutal Selection Process

Delta Force has a brutal selection program, and it is one of legend. Just like the British Special Air Service(SAS), they test their candidates mentally and physically to their absolute limits. Once they reach those limits, they take them a long way beyond those limits and teach them to be comfortable in the most extreme situations imaginable.

WHY DELTA OPERATORS ARE UNIQUE

9

PART 2 - The Difference Between Delta ,SEAL Team SIX and Other Units

Before we get to Delta Force and SEAL Team Six let's look at the funnel that leads to both units:

The United States Special Operations Command (USSOCOM or SOCOM).

SOCOM is the umbrella organization in charge of running all the special operations capabilities of all the services. This includes the Army, Marine Corps, Navy, and Air Force. All the services run independently but SOCOM is the coordinating organization to optimize and enhance the capabilities of the of US Special Operations. SOCOM is very important in terms of combining the strengths of the different services and their specialties to reach mission objectives.

Let's look at the unit structures of first SOCOM and secondly JSOC.

The United States Special Operations Command (USSOCOM or SOCOM)

-Army
- 1st Special Forces Command (Airborne) (Also Known As Green Berets)
- 75th Ranger Regiment (An Elite Specialised Light-infantry Unit)

-Marine Corps
- Marine Raider Regiment

-Navy
- US Navy SEALs

-Air Force
- Combat Controllers
- Pararescuemen

- Special Operations Weather Technicians

Joint Special Operations Command (JSOC)

The Joint Special Operations Command (JSOC) is a command structure of the Elite Special Forces groups in the US Military. JSOC purpose is to execute the most important military objectives of the US Military.

JSOC consists of the following groups:
- **The Army**- Delta Force
- **Navy** - SEAL TEAM SIX
- **Air Force** - 24th Special Tactics Squadron

These units are also sometimes referred to as "Tier One Units".

Sometimes support units Units from the Army's 75th Ranger Regiment and 160th Special Operations Aviation Regiment is attached to JSOC in a supporting capacity.

SEAL TEAM SIX is the tip of the spear of the US NAVY. They are trained and equipped to deal with any and all situations. SEAL TEAM SIX and DELTA Force are the US military's primary counter-terrorism forces.

Now Let's Look At Some Differences between SEAL Team SIX and DELTA:

(1)Recruitment and Selection
 SEAL TEAM SIX recruits only within the SEAL Teams. That means every recruit is already a Navy SEAL. Being a SEAL is already a major achievement but believe it or not, SEAL TEAM SIX is one step up.

Delta Force Recruits mainly from the Special Forces(Green Berets) and the 75th Ranger Regiment. However, the Delta Force also recruits from the Marine Corps, Air Force, and Coast Gaurd. Navy Seals also have the option of going to Delta Force selection. Delta Force values the variety of backgrounds of its members and sees the differences as an asset.

Most recruits will not make it through the selection of both units. Only about 10% of candidates make it through Delta and SEAL TEAM Six Selections. Both units have a totally different selection and organization, but both are brutal in nature.

(2)Missions

Both units have similar missions. Both units do hostage rescue and counter-terrorism. Both units also do direct action and special reconnaissance against high-value targets.

Although DELTA has troops that conduct maritime missions it's not their specialty.SEAL TEAM SIX for obvious reasons conduct specialized maritime operations.

(3)Culture

The culture within the units is a big difference.SEAL Team SIX still has the SEAL TEAM culture and heritage.

DELTA FORCE is the pioneers in the USA for this type of small specialized unit of Specially trained Operators than can work alone or in small groups anywhere in the world. The British SAS started it and Delta was modeled after them. Some are of the opinion that Delta has even gone up a level due to the dynamic culture within the Delta Detachment.

Delta also has a unique culture due to its mixed background of its members. Delta values its diversity in background and this gives DELTA FORCE an edge in terms of unpredictability. Delta values independent thinking and adaptability.

Delta Force has its roots in the Elite British Special Air Service(SAS) and this lineage is an incredible strength in Delta Force.

Part 2 of this Book

In Part 2 of this book, I will go into more details of the Special Forces(Green Berets), Navy SEALs and SAS. It's important to have insight into these units to have a better understanding of Delta Force and how it all fits together.

10

GREEN BERETS

Who Are The Green Berets?

The Special Forces is an elite squad considered to have some of the most experienced fighters in the world. They are referred to as Green

Berets due to their special head gear, although many people somehow confuse them with the Army Rangers and Navy SEALs.

Just like any other special operation group in the United States, the Green Berets are known in Latin as "Sine Pari," which means "Without Equal". The troop has adopted its own motto that is "To Free the Oppressed," or "De Oppresso Liber".

This motto is a dedicated call to duty and not just what any other military group could live up to. This special calling explains the reason behind the Special Forces' exploits as elaborated in countless books, movies, and music.

Historical Beginnings

The Green Berets were founded during the World War II when the need to perform missions that do not fit any military categorized mission became apparent. In 1952, Brigadier General Robert McClure and two other Army Officers were granted permission by the US government to recruit and create a specialized army to carry out highly classified and specialized missions for the United States. In 1953, the first batch of Green Berets was deployed.

In 1961, President John F. Kennedy praised the Green Berets for their impressive skills and capabilities. He said that they are "a symbol of excellence, a badge of courage, a mark of distinction in the fight for freedom." When the president was assassinated, the Green Berets drew a black line on the brim of their berets to honor the fallen president. This black line on the brim of their beret became a permanent fixture in their uniforms.

President John F. Kennedy was also honored by the Green Berets by naming the special unit in charge of training new recruits as John F.

Kennedy Special Warfare Center. To date, the Green Berets pay their respects to President Kennedy by putting a wreath on his gravesite every year.

Since they are special operations units, they report directly to US-SOCOM, a geographic combatant command, or related authorities of command. This is opposed to other forces that work under command authority of the ground commanders in the countries they are operating.

Due to their level of expertise, the Special Operations Group (SOG) and the highly secretive Special Activities Division (SAD) get their recruits from these forces. The two groups are part of the United States Central Intelligence Agency (CIA).

The US Special Forces Tasks

The Green Berets are extremely qualified in terms of military skills, various multi-national cultures and languages in addition to being the best in unconventional warfare. The team members in the Special Forces work as a unit, relying on each other in various situations for long duration's of time. Thus, they easily form close relationships with long-standing personal ties.

The US Special Forces are mainly tasked with five major missions. Although their main mission is to handle unconventional warfare, they also handle counter terrorism, offer special reconnaissance, direct action, and foreign internal defense. From these roles, foreign internal defense and unconventional warfare emphasize language, cultural factors along with training skills when working hand in hand with foreign troops. The missions are briefly explained here:

- **Counterterrorism**

The Green Berets are deployed to prevent, take necessary action and to resolve incidents of terrorism abroad. Apart from deterring and responding to terrorist activities, the army officers often train other countries military about the basics of countering terrorism. Current goals that the special forces group try to meet is stopping terrorists before they strike, as well as preventing the formation of terror cells.

- **Real World Missions**

The Green Berets are often deployed to undertake missions against terrorism to counter terror attacks in a number of situations. The troops have often worked with other nations allies since the attack on the World Trade Center in New York. They have disassembled terrorist cells, facilitated the capture of a number of al-Qaeda members, and even interrupted the funding of such terror groups. These soldiers do work with local police forces and governments to detect and crack down on the rapidly growing terror groups globally.

- **Direct Action**

Most of these are usually short duration strikes that come in handy when the Green Berets want to seize, capture, recover and damage the weapons of the enemies. They also undertake the direct action in order to destroy information or recover designated material or personnel.

- **Foreign Internal Defense**

They are meant to plan, assist and offer training to the military and the defense forces of foreign governments as well as to protect the citizens of these nations from aggressions.

- **Special Reconnaissance**

This is a combination of special roles that involve gathering intelligence in order to monitor the movements of the enemy and their operations.

- **Unconventional Warfare**

The green berets have often adopted the guerilla warfare also known as Unconventional Warfare or UW for various missions. Such missions include training, equipping, advising and helping the forces in the enemy-controlled or enemy-held zones.

Other roles of the special forces is doing manhunts, security assistance, physiological operations, peace keeping, information operations, humanitarian demining, humanitarian assistance, rescuing of hostages, counter-proliferation, counter narcotics and combat search and rescue.

Operations may range from working as bodyguards to an Eastern European leader to giving advise to Afghani tribal chief on consolidating his power. Actually, you never get to detect their presence not until they successfully undertake their mission. Thus, they are the first line of defense globally.

This special group works with little oversight, and serves native people in their areas of operations (AOs) operating as "warrior-diplomats." Though their role is to offer support to US interests, the Special Forces do exist in the haze that seem to float between groups and people, country and other nations and such like.

The soldiers are grouped into 12-man teams referred to as Operational Detachment Alpha or ODAs. In this team, each ODA has its own attitude, own culture and way of operating. The team is flexible and versatile to allow shifting of gears between various missions, deployments and environments.

Special Forces Wartime Duties

Most of their missions or operations are carried out during the actual war, where both conventional and unconventional techniques are employed. The conventional warfare strategies include military operations that are undertaken on a massive scale. Such techniques involve use of tanks, large troop forces, ships, planes and other advanced weapons.

On the other hand, unconventional techniques often involve guerrilla warfare, which is a fight that isn't staged and is done as a surprise. Such war comprises uprisings or insurgencies, precise fast-strikes and other bush-like tactics that still make a huge impact. This kind of technique is well understood by these Special Forces as it helps them attack from both without and within. With this technique, they can easily penetrate the battle zone and make insurgencies from within the territory of the enemy.

Guerrilla warfare is highly risky work. Therefore, Green Berets must operate on their own for long durations and make their own decisions. They need to live and act as locals do, and even interact with them to get their trust and required information. Members often work without uniform, a situation that excludes them from Geneva Convention protection, which makes them vulnerable. The Geneva treaty outlines the roles of a combatant during war along with the right accorded to him. Under this global treaty, a soldier not in uniform is unprotected. Therefore, a Green Beret can be killed or tortured without any assistance especially if detected by enemy combatant.

Once into the territory of the enemy, the Special Forces identify people unhappy with the current living condition or power struggles. The disaffected groups could be native or local communities being oppressed by the current government, or can be minority groups or former people on power. The Special Forces do consolidate the people into one force to facilitate enemies to be fought guerrilla style. The grouping is referred to as multiplying of forces. For instance, Green Berets team consolidated a 60,000-member guerrilla army to combat the enemy during the Vietnam War.

The army that the Special Forces accumulate behind the enemy lines is trained, equipped and follows their guidance and command. The troops do their best to obtain as much intelligence as possible about the enemy and even spread propaganda. In other cases, they interrupt the information systems owned by the enemies through military strikes on the communication equipment. As the Green Berets are undetectable and can "vanish instantly", they are skilled in identifying targets for the conventional army. A good example was in Afghanistan when the Special Forces selected the targets that would make the biggest impact for US missiles.

Skills You Need To Become A Green Beret

Joining the Green Berets

To join this prestigious group of men, one has to undergo a very rigorous and diverse training. The training take a long time to complete so it can take years before you can call yourself a Green Beret.

The qualifications for joining the Green Berets are also a little bit different from regular soldiers. Most men who join the Green Berets have college level education, some even with post graduate degrees.

Within the ranks of existing soldiers, the Green Berets allow volunteers to join the program if their rank is Private First Class or higher for the enlisted and Captain or higher for the officers. Regular men who are not in any military service can also join.

In order to become a Green Beret, you need to not only be able to do a hundred pushups, but you also have to be intelligent, have an excellent record of previous military service for around 3 years, and be highly motivated. However, based on the new program, you can skip the 3 years wait and go straight to the SFAS immediately after Army Boot Camp.

In order to be physically prepared for each phase of training, you need to perform a number of workouts. Ability to workout properly can help you learn the skills needed for the advanced training.

Getting Into SFAS

The initial requirement is to pass the Special Forces Assessment and Selection Course (SFAS) by achieving a minimum of 260. The course involves basic physical fitness on the Army physical fitness test. If ready for applying for this course, remember the training is extremely selective and competitive.

You can't settle for minimum score in anything! Just work towards these goals:

*Run a 2-mile distance in 12-14 minutes

*Complete 100 push-ups in 2 minutes

*Do 100 sit-ups in 2 minutes

Achieving these goals allows you to get a score of 300 thus increase chances for your selection for training.

The Q Course

Once done with selection, you are meant to attend a 'Q course', which takes 6-12 months based on your qualifications. You train daily, starting early and ending late, thus your attitude should be of a marathoner. You should be ready for the long exercises and maintain your ability to focus amid stress and fatigue accompanied by the training. If really aiming to excel in Green Berets training, you should have the following skills:

- **1. Swimming:**

*Be able to swim 2-3 times weekly, for a distance of 1000-2000 meters every time.

*Be able to swim 1 day a week while wearing boots for 100 meters

*Be able to swim when wearing fins at least half of the time.

- **2. Running skills:**

*Able to complete 3-5 miles four to five times a week as fast as possible

*Ability to do rucksack marches 2 times a week when carrying 30-50 pound load, and march 5-15 miles at a fast walking pace.

- **3. PT: Everyday skills:**

*Able to do sit-ups with 200-300 repetitions; for 5-10 sets of 40-50 reps

*Should manage doing push-ups, 75-100 repetitions; 7-10 sets of 10 reps

*Push-ups, 200-300 repetitions; 10-15 sets of 20 reps

Special Forces Training - The Q Course

To be eligible for Green Beret training, soldiers should have undergone

Basic Combat Training and the Advanced Individualized Training at the U.S. Airborne School. Other requirements that you need to qualify for Special Forces training include:

- 1. Be a 20-30 years old male and a high school graduate
- 2. Be a citizen of the United States of America.
- 3. Have General Technical score of at least 107 and have attained a combat operation score of 98 in the Armed Services Vocational Aptitude Battery
- 4. Be qualified or be a volunteer for airborne training
- 5. Have scored at least 60 point on each of the events, with a total minimum score of 240 based on the Army Physical Fitness Test
- 6. Qualify for the "SECRET" security clearance.
- 7. Able to swim about 50 meters while wearing boots
- 8. Must have a 20/20 or corrected to the same in both near and distant vision in all eyes.
- 9. Have completed the Pre-Basic Task list successfully
- 10. Meet the fitness standard as prescribed in the AR 40-501

It's also recommended to be bilingual although you would be trained on language, culture, customs, tradition and the geography of the area you would serve as your Areas of Operation (AO).

The training that you have to undergo before you become a Green Beret is called Special Forces Qualification Course (SFQC) or simply the Q Course. It starts with a 30-day preparation course followed by the Special Forces Assessment and Selection (SFAS).

Becoming a Green Beret is hard. The qualification into the group is highly restrictive, and the training is usually rigorous. The training often begins with a 30-day preparation course referred to as SOPC (Special Operations Preparation Course). This course is meant to assist the already trained soldiers to be more ready to the forthcoming physical and mental stress.

The preparation course involves a lot of physical and mental endurance tests that are made to prepare you for an even tougher training under the SFAS. These include going through obstacle courses, calisthenics, marching and running for hours and land navigation. The training sometimes starts during the wee hours of the morning when the volunteers have only had very little sleep and in the worst conditions possible.

After the preparation course, the training for SFAS will begin. This is on the premise that you completed the preparation course and passed. During the SFAS, the training endured by the volunteers include some of the toughest tasks that a person can go through. These tasks are made to test the physical, mental, and psychological capacity of the person. It is during this period that a lot of volunteers get cut because they are not able to withstand the training.

After the month of preparation, a 24-day long selection process follows, referred to as SFAS (Special Forces Assessment and Selection). This course is aimed at rooting out the less-confident soldiers from those able to complete the program. Recruits are assessed in terms of their survival skills, and are put into a stronger preparation for intense physical and mental training.

The preparation course is meant to test the endurance and mental and physical capability of the individual. The SFAS tests the volunteers on how they work as a team. During the SFAS, you are divided into teams of 12. In order to succeed, you must work with your team to complete a series of tasks that are exhausting, grueling and arduous. the tasks that volunteers are made undergo include heavy lifting, swimming on waters with extremely cold temperatures, rescue missions, land navigation, and getting out of mentally taxing situations to name a few. You could get seriously hurt during the training.

Test of Mind, Body, and Resolve

Because the Green Berets take on missions that are unusual or out of the ordinary, the training that they undergo are designed to make them think on their feet and use items that are on hand to complete the mission. The training are patterned after real life situations like being held captive by the enemy or being tortured to give up information. Retired members of the Green Berets have disclosed that they went through tests that include being beaten or tortured and were made to try and get out of these situations.

The SFAS also include a series of mental and logical tests like IQ tests, Defense Language Aptitude Battery test that the volunteers also have to pass on top of the physical training. The final test is an endurance test where the volunteers are made to march 32 miles non-stop and other simulations of real life work that a Green Beret undergoes.

Students who do not get in the Q Course fall into 3 categories:

- 1. Those who quit without finishing the course or have voluntarily withdrawn are designated NTR or Not-to-Return. This means what it says, your career with the US Army Special Forces ends here.
- 2. Soldiers who are not injured critically are permitted to return to the course once able.
- 3. Candidates that completed the course but are not selected are given the chance to retake the selection again after 12 to 24 months.

Once you have completed and passed the SFAS, you will then train for the specific Areas of Operations or AOs and will begin formal training in the Special Forces Qualifications Course (SFQC). The AOs selected could be the place you will eventually be assigned.

These are the AOs that the Green Berets operate in:

- - U.S. European Command - Africa, Western and Eastern Europe, North Asia
- - U.S. Northern Command - All of North America up to the Arctic Circle and Northern Central America
- - U.S. Pacific Command South - Asia, Australia, Greenland, Indochina, all Pacific Islands
- - U.S. Southern Command - Central and South America and the Caribbean
- - U.S. Central Command - Northeast Africa, the Middle East and part of Eurasia

Scope of the Q Course

During this training, recruits are exposed to all conditions and treatments they should encounter once in enemy territory. They are hooded, mistreated, blindfolded and pushed to the breaking point.

Recruits are cross-trained in a wide variety of skills to be able to fill for each other while in combat. Each skill is important and the combination yields a highly specialized Special Forces unit or detachment.

Training under the Q Course include SERE (Survival, Evasion, Resistance and Escape), weapons and combat training, land and sea navigation, survival, parachuting and scuba diving. Language and cultural training is also included in this course. Emphasis will always be placed on how to think on your feet.

Foreign languages will be taught to recruits making them multilingual.

You will also be trained in a particular specialty that you excel in and that could support cross training in other specialties. This ensures that in case one member of the team is unable to perform his role, the other members of the team can back him up. Most Green Berets have at least 2 specialties that he is an expert in.

Because the Green Berets' missions are non-conventional, training are given for all sorts of situations. Training problem analysis and resolution take up the most number of hours during the Q Course. Unconventional weapons training and obtaining counterintelligence are also some of the specialized training given to Green Berets. These days counter-terrorism training and obtaining intelligence on terrorists has also become a part of their training.

After passing the Q Course, a graduation ceremony is given to the successful recruits. This is where the students get to wear their green beret for the first time.

Moving On After The Q Course

Once you are fully trained, you will be grouped in a team composed of 12 members. These are usually the team you passed the Q Course with. Within the 12 man team or the detachment structure, you will fill a specialized role that one other member of the team can fill in in case you are compromised in battle or in any way unable to fulfill your role. These teams are called the Alpha Team or the A-team.

There are two leadership roles within the A-team, and these are the Commanding Officer and the Warrant Officer, which is the second in command. The remaining 10 members of the team will be assigned to five specialist positions so that each team will have two persons specializing in one position. This kind of structure makes it easier to divide the team into smaller groups of 6 in case the need arises.

The 5 specialist positions and 2 leadership positions that a fully trained Green Beret can hold within the A-team are as follows:

1. Commanding Officer

The Commanding Officer is the highest ranked Green Beret within the detachment unit. He is responsible for leading the group, cascading the nature of the mission to the team, and leading the team through the mission in the best possible way.

2. Warrant Officer

A Warrant Officer, as mentioned earlier, is the second in command within the A-Team. He is responsible for the other half of the team in case there will be a need to divide them into smaller groups of 6. He is also trained in the ways that a Commanding Officer is trained and can take over the whole team in case the Commanding Officer is unable to perform his duties.

3. Communications Sergeants

Communications Sergeants are specialists trained in handling highly sophisticated communications equipment and are responsible for taking care of the equipment so that they don't fall into the wrong hands. They are also well trained in broadcasting psychological operations if needed. They are responsible for transmitting intelligence learned from the enemies to the Special Operations Command (SOCOM). In the battlefield, the Communications Sergeants carry the extra weight of these communications equipment.

4. Intelligence and Operations Sergeants

In the movies, there is always that one person who seems to know everything about the enemy. They are the ones who scout the location, watch the enemies, and generally get intelligence on what the enemies are up to. They provide the team with the needed information about the enemies before they go into battle. They are also the ones responsible for identifying what sort of equipment the team will need in a particular mission.

5. Medical Officers

Medical Officers are trained medical doctors and soldiers at the same time. They have been called "walking hospitals" on some instances as they are able to perform basic surgery, do consultations, give diagnosis, perform dental procedures, suture wounds, treat burns, and handle all other medical problems that a soldier can encounter during battle. Medical officers immersed in a particular AO can set up clinics and even treat locals while he is there. Medical Officers have 10 additional months of training after he has completed the regular Green Beret training.

6. Weapons Sergeants

Weapons Sergeants are trained in the use of all sorts of weapons including the weapons used in the AO they are stationed in. They can also provide weapons training to other people in case an army is needed.

7. Engineer Sergeants

Engineer Sergeants are the go to guys when it comes to logistics. They are the navigators of the team. They lead the team through terrains and can build makeshift passage like bridges in case there is none.

Within the A-team, one group of 6 people is specially trained for airborne insertion while the other is trained in underwater insertion. But all 12 members of the team are trained in ground infiltration.

The duties of the Green Berets can be classified into 3 categories. These are wartime operations, post-hostility or peacetime operations, and humanitarian missions.

Wartime operations are generally aimed at stopping the war. Post hostility or peacetime operations aims to prevent war from erupting. Lastly, humanitarian missions are missions that aim to help the AOs by providing medical care, training locals on self-defense and delivering relief goods to areas devastated by war and calamities. Because Green Berets' mission is to be immersed into the AOs they are assigned to, their humanitarian missions help them gain the trust and cooperation of the locals.

Green Berets also serve as advisers to political leaders and can lead non government organizations (NGOs) while stationed in their particular AOs. Their highly specialized training also makes them perfect trainers for other soldiers as well.

Other Courses

After raking in countless hours of training and completing the Q Course, a Green Beret is ready to take on missions. Some of these graduates prefer to take up specialized training after they complete the Q Course. These courses are more advanced skills training that build upon existing Green Beret training.

These are some of the courses you can take after completing the Q Course:

1. Military Free Fall Parachutist Course

2. Combat Diver Qualification Course

3. Special Forces Sniper Course

4. Special Forces Master Mountaineer Course

5. Chemical Recon Detachment Training

The road to becoming a Green Beret is a long, arduous and tough road. You must be physically, mentally and emotionally fit in order to pass. Sometimes even the best still fail one way or another. You must be ready for all sorts of situations and be fully committed to anything that the US Army Special Forces assigns to you. Do you think you have what it takes?

Recent Special Forces Operations

The U.S Special Forces has been conducting various military combat operations since the September 11 terrorist attacks. The Green Berets started major action at Vietnam to train Vietnamese soldiers to fight guerrilla war and counter-insurgency tactics. The troop later trained troops to fight insurgencies in places such as Colombia and El Salvador. More recent operations were in Yemen, Philippines and Somalia in attempt to train locals and combat insurgent Islamists.

The recent major operation carried out by Green Berets is at Nerkh district of Afghanistan that lies west of Kabul to fight the Taliban. The soldiers, trained to conduct unconventional warfare were installed into various areas to hunt the insurgents and strengthen the resolve of national government forces. Special Forces located at Chamkani hiked hundreds of miles to combat insurgents from Pakistan, who use the area to smuggle fighters, arms and explosives.

In retaliation, the insurgents responded through several attacks on the Chamkani military base. Since the arrival of the Green Berets in Afghanistan, the base has been attacked with 120 rockets and mortars, which makes it the most targeted military base in the country. In a single month, more than 5 attacks were witnessed, whereas rockets would explode and set ablaze parts of the base. A sergeant with the Green Beret termed the operation similar to shooting a fish in a fish bowl, with them "being the fish".

The army often worked with Afghan commandos in their regular missions into the valley to combat the insurgents. In one attack, the SF solders were able to kill over 25 insurgents, a toll that conventional forces never achieve in a single fight.

Apart from guerrilla warfare, the Green Berets in March 2015 operated the pilot-less reconnaissance drones to assist the Lebanese army combat the ISIS among other extremist groups in Lebanon. Such support is part of military help that includes provision of weapons and ammunition to the local forces.

Role Of Special Forces Against Terrorism

Green Berets have often conducted surveillance and reconnaissance on terrorists' activities, connections, infrastructures, and facilities. The Special Forces use long range devices among them cameras, telescope and other advanced intelligence to collect information. The data obtained is analyzed to help plan, support and conduct special operations tasks. From this data, the Special Forces can then carry out direct action against the terrorists.

Common combat operations include raids, assaults and ambushes on terrorists' facilities, persons or groups. Direct action activities include capture of designated materials or personnel, recovery of any captured personnel and designate targets for military action. The targets are identified through laser designators for precision guided ammunitions such as the "SMART bombs"

Special Forces also offer military assistance to countries targeted by terrorists. Military assistance includes training, advice and assisting allied soldiers. These tasks are however not listed as the core objectives of the Special Forces, yet they have positively affected countering terrorism. The forces also play a vital role in a number of global military combat missions led by the EU or NATO.

Challenges and criticisms

The greatest challenge encountered by Special Forces in carrying out counter-terrorist measures is the complaints and warnings of civil liberties. These groups often allege that such actions often target the innocent citizens as well as detainees from States attempting to fight terror. Such measures are often viewed as abuses of power or to some extent as violations of human rights, as opposed to being aimed at tightening security. The other challenge is that counter-terrorism systems are big in physical terms ranging from long boarders to vast areas, political interferences and degree of terrorism threats.

11

NAVY SEALS

The SEALs are the primary special operations force of the United States Navy. They are also a part the US Special Operations Command (USSOCOM) and the Naval Special Warfare Command. Their name stands for United States Navy's Sea, Air, and Land Teams (SE from sea,

A from Air, and L from Land). They are named such because they are sent to conduct missions whether on the sea, air, or land. Aside from this, they are also expected to operate in places of extreme conditions such as tropical jungles, fiery arid deserts, and frozen lands. In order to prepare them for this, their training is highly specialized and extreme (more on this in a later chapter).

The SEALs, like other units of the military, are trained and equipped for combat. However, the main difference is that they are assigned to special warfare. Their duty is composed of small-unit military missions of a maritime nature. Small-unit means the mission is usually carried out by a single individual or just a pair, but there are also missions where a platoon of up to 16 is sent. These missions commence from and return to a coastline, delta, swamp, ocean, or river. SEALs can take on operations that require going through shallow waters, where submarines and deep-draft ships are not ideal, or outright can't go through, because of the limited depth. SEALs may have been, historically speaking, deployed from the waters but today, they can perform equivalently well from the land and the air.

The nature of SEAL missions is mostly covert – the team gets in, performs the task, and gets out quickly without being detected. Because of this, each mission is planned in extreme detail, and the sent team must execute it in a precise manner. This is partly why even US citizens only hear of SEAL operations in the news after their success.

The primary tasks of SEALs are specific and/or have high strategic value. These include:

- Direct action. This is to assault specific target/s. The targets are usually high-priority ones and always have a strong strategic value. For example, taking out an enemy leader.

- Counter-terrorism. This is combating terrorist operations whether stopping actual terrorist operations or taking preventive measures. This also involves the protection of civilian citizens and military personnel and installations.

- Unconventional warfare. Teams perform so-called guerilla tactics – where a small and mobile combat group carries out battle methods outside direct confrontation. Some examples of this are strategic ambush of enemy units, creating diversions, destroying the enemy's supplies, and enemy base demolitions.

- Special reconnaissance. This is to gather intelligence regarding an environment or enemy movements, or both. This also includes other types of surveillance whether covert or overt. The gathered information is meant to aid in further missions, like establishing ideal entry and exit points, identifying hazards, and pinpointing a target's location.

- Foreign internal defense. In order to build good international relationships, SEALs train foreign nationals. They may also perform or aid in other specific missions for other objectives when necessary, and no other military units are specialized to conduct. Some examples are:Personnel recovery,Hostage rescue,Hydrographic Reconnaissance,Counter-drug operations.

During the times when SEALs are not deployed on missions, they are constantly in training. They refine basic skills and acquire new skills. This is both to keep them in prime condition and learn more techniques and skills that would ensure success in actual operations.

History of the US Navy SEALs

The roots of the US Navy SEALs can be traced back to World War II. Groups called Naval Combat Demolition Units (NCDUs) were formed. The need for these teams was realized because of Japan's attack on Pearl Harbor in 1941.

The US military needed to invade Japan from the sea, but there were hazards, particularly attacks from concealed enemies and landmines. So, the US Navy formed the NCDUs. These were teams comprised of six men. Their task was to safely arrive on enemy shores, clear obstacles, to create a path, and gather enemy and location intelligence which they'll bring back to the main body of troops.

The NCDUs underwent special training in order to perform these tasks. Developing physical strength composed a huge portion of their training.

They would carry heavy loads, swim, run, and move within small boats.

Another part of the training is handling explosives. In 1943, the US military further realized the need for hydrographic reconnaissance as well as more underwater demolitions. This was due to the landing of the US Marines on Tarawa Atoll in the South Pacific.

Aside from enemy threats, amphibious landings faced problems caused by nature. The islands on the said atoll have treacherous tides, and their reefs are shallow. Naval transport vessels just can't go through them. One time, the Marines were able to send in one wave of Marines through, but the second wave was hindered by a low tide. So, the troops unloaded and waded through the water to reach the shore. Doing so was physically exhausting and made them vulnerable to enemy attacks. The majority of them were either killed or drowned before they reached the shore. Meanwhile, the Marines who got through were being overwhelmed by the enemy on the beach because the support from the second wave never came. This overwhelming defeat was a costly lesson that surely no Navy would want to repeat. Resources were wasted and, more tragically, many American fighting men lost their lives. Hence, a program for demolitions training was commissioned. The NCDU evolved into the Underwater Demolition Teams (UDT).

Nicknamed "frogmen," the UDTs proved extremely effective in several amphibious battles, notably in the Korean War. They swam to the shore and cleared obstacles, giving way to the amphibious invasion by the main body of troops. In addition, they also blew up strategic targets such as tunnels and bridges.

During the 1960s, President John F. Kennedy declared that small teams composed of guerilla fighters needed to be sent to wage low-intensity conflict in what later came to be known as the Vietnam War. The US ally South Vietnam needed help in the fight against the Soviet ally North Vietnam. The army already had its elite team of Special Forces, more popularly known as the Green Berets. Hence, the Navy found the need to form their own unit for Special Operations. With the UDT training program as a foundation, the US Navy SEALs were born. They were sent in to perform guerilla operations – going behind enemy lines to destroy enemy supplies, raid enemy bases, sabotage communication, and obliterate stored ammunitions. Prepared by their training, the teams became extremely effective in traversing Vietnam's rivers, coasts, and jungles.

While some battles were won because of SEAL missions, the Vietnam War proved to be a lost cause for the United States as they were unable to prevent the communists from taking over the country. Due to this, the budget for the military was diminished causing many of the Special Forces units to be downsized or even inactivated completely. However, the SEALs' success in missions validated their worth several times over. From then on, the SEALs continued to train and were sent on many missions of great significance.

Volunteering and Requirements

Enlisting for Navy SEAL training is purely voluntary. Before anyone can volunteer, though, there are many requirements. Being a soldier in any combat military unit already has extreme demands, but as you have seen, the nature of SEAL missions imposes even greater demands.

A person who wishes to volunteer for SEAL training must meet the following requirements:

- The volunteer must be on active duty with the US Navy.
- The volunteer must be male (Contrary to what is portrayed in the film G.I. Jane starring Demi Moore, women are not allowed to undergo Navy SEAL training.).
- Age must be less than or equal to 28. However, individuals of 29 or 30 years may be accepted with a special waiver.
- Vision should be at least 20/40 in one eye and at least 20/70 in the other. It is possible to acquire corrective surgery.
- The volunteer must be a citizen of the United States.
- The volunteer must pass the Armed Services Vocational Aptitude Battery (ASVAB) test.

The volunteer must pass a rigorous physical screening. The procedure for this screening is as follows:

- Swimming: complete 500 yards within 12.5 minutes.

10-minute rest

- Push-ups: complete 42 within two minutes.

2-minute rest

- Sit-ups: complete 50 within two minutes.

2-minute rest

- Pull-ups: complete 6

10-minute rest

- Running: complete 1.5 miles while wearing long pants and boots within 11.5 minutes

Passing the requirements is just the start. It only qualifies the volunteer for training. He is not yet a SEAL, but rather a potential SEAL. The volunteer must complete the training in order to become a fully qualified SEAL.

Difficulty Level

Like any military training, SEAL training is highly meticulous. This may not be already a given, but that's because lives are at stake when in real operations. Each SEAL must be ready to deal with any potential situation. SEAL training is reputed to be one of the most difficult, if not the most difficult, military training regimens in the world. With a drop-out rate that sometimes exceeds 90% per class, meeting the requirements is apparently the easy part.

There is a certain part in SEAL training that many people refer to as "Hell Week" (more on this later). The term might not be an exaggeration. The things they undergo are brutal, to say the least. The process is long too. Before a SEAL is deemed ready for deployment, it may take more than two years.

SEAL selection is not designed to get you fit. If you pass the requirements, particularly the screening, you are already in shape. The training aims to take the candidates beyond that. It can even be said that being in shape is just a minimum requirement to stand a chance at surviving the training.

Each event in training is called " evolution." The term is pretty apt since the training seems to make the trainees evolve. At the very least, it pushes them to the limits of human capabilities both physically and mentally. It has been shown by science that SEALs and people with similar military training have resistances to extreme cold and heat way higher than the average human.

Furthermore, their performance for combat and other tasks aren't diminished even with a certain amount of exposure to harsh elements.

Their strength, dexterity, focus, stamina, reflexes, and other important characteristics for a soldier are all at the upper limits.

One might wonder why SEAL training is conducted with such a high degree of difficulty. Does it have to be that harsh? The short answer is yes. As you might have noticed in the first chapter, SEALs face harsh conditions when they are sent to operations, and they aren't sent there just to survive. They must thrive. They have missions. They have tasks to perform. They shouldn't just withstand the stresses but also keep their focus in order to fulfill their missions.

Another reason for this difficulty level is to meticulously filter the SEAL candidates. The drop-out rate is indeed high, as mentioned earlier. The men who emerge successfully from the training must be able to handle virtually anything that comes their way in order to perform the job at hand. This includes demolitions, navigation, armed and unarmed combat, diving, combat swimming, and parachuting. They are expected to perform these tasks even under the intense mental and physical pressure of any environment that the mission entails. Those who can not endure these stresses during the training (wherein no lives at stake) are not likely to be able to endure them in actual operations (wherein lives are really on the line). If they are sent to missions, chances are good that they will just be sent to die or get other friendly personnel killed.

The SEAL Training

So then, what exactly do SEAL trainees go through?

Preparatory

The battle cry of the US Navy SEALs is "Hooyah!" and if you witness a training session, you will hear it a lot from the trainees. This becomes instilled in them as an automatic response that can mean many things. But commonly, it would mean "understood," "yes," or "this evolution can't beat me!" (Remember that evolution is the term for any single event in a training schedule.)

Before anything else, the teamwork mindset is taught to SEAL trainees from the very start of training. The belief within the US Navy SEAL regards teamwork with great importance. Throughout history, SEALs have never left behind another SEAL on a mission. This is a fact that serves as a demonstration of their focus on teamwork. This is built up and further instilled on the minds of SEALs throughout the training and beyond. They continuously learn why teamwork is vital to the nature of work they'll be performing. SEALs carry out jobs that might not be doable for a single individual, but can be done by a team comprised of men who possess the same skills. The better they can work as a team, the higher their chances of success.

The Naval Special Warfare Prep School is the first part of the formal training for SEAL candidates. This is an 8-week period where the ways of the Navy SEALs get drilled into the trainees, including the above-mentioned concepts. This is where the volunteers truly get to understand what they are entering.

BUD/S

After the Prep School, the trainees who make the grade and wish to continue move on to the Basic Underwater Demolition/SEAL (BUD/S) training, a 24-week period divided into different phases: indoctrination, basic conditioning, SCUBA training, and land-warfare training.

In the indoctrination phase, potential SEALs still have it relatively easy. They are introduced to the performances and techniques required for the later phases of the BUD/S. More importantly, this phase prepares them mentally and physically for what's to come. Yes, the Prep School is not deemed to be enough preparation. Indoctrination lasts five weeks.

Basic Conditioning Phase

The next phase is Basic Conditioning. This is where the fun starts, if "fun" means "going gets rough" for you. It might have "basic" in its name, but that didn't make the phase any easier. In fact, this part of the training is where the most number of Drops on Request (DOR) are submitted (i.e. where most candidates decide to drop out). For eight weeks, trainees run, swim, exercise without special equipment (calisthenics), and taught small-boat operations. Each day of those weeks, two events are constant: a one to two-mile swim and completion of perhaps the most difficult obstacle course known to man. Both of these events are always timed, and each trainee is expected to break his own record every day.

Another significant component of Basic Conditioning is drownproofing – so called because this evolution involves trainees learning to swim while both of their hands and feet are bound. It's not just simple swimming either. To make the grade for this event, a potential SEAL must complete the following steps (in a 9 feet pool):

1. Bob – five minutes
2. Float – five minutes as well
3. Swim – for 100 meters
4. Bob – two minutes
5. Perform flips – forward and backward
6. Swim to the pool's bottom and retrieve one item using his teeth
7. Swim back to the surface
8. Bob – five minutes again

One more notable evolution is called surf torture (also known as "cold water conditioning") where perhaps the SEALs develop most of their resistance to cold. The trainees are exposed to waters with a temperature range of 65 to 68 degrees Fahrenheit (or 18 to 20 degrees Celsius). After being submerged, the trainees may be ordered to perform some calisthenics or run 1.5 miles along the beach – whichever the case, they must do it while wearing their wet clothes and footwear. After that, they will be ordered to submerge on the surf again.

In the drills during the Basic Conditioning phase, the potential SEALs are divided into teams, each of which is assigned a rubber boat – an inflatable Zodiac. In many of these drills, each team is required to carry their own Zodiac as they move from one task to the next.

The Hell Week

Deserving of special mention in the BUD/S basic conditioning phase is the Hell Week. This happens during the fourth week of the phase. This period is comprised of five days and five nights. The potential SEALs continuously train throughout that period, and they'll only sleep for a total of four hours maximum. That's right – four hours out of the five days and five nights. The trainees go through a barrage of evolutions. They are given four meals per day – generally hot meals, eat-all-you-can. Sometimes, the meals are MREs though. The hot meals serve as a replacement for warmth and dryness. Moreover, the meals provide some psychological motivation for the sleep-deprived trainees – a motivation that they definitely need.

Almost all the evolutions carried out within Hell Week require the teams to carry their respective Zodiacs above their heads. There will be timed exercises, mud crawling, and runs distributed throughout the duration.

The majority of dropping out occurs during the Hell Week.

These rigorous training procedures are not just necessary – they are critical to a Navy SEAL's performance in actual operations. They need to achieve a mind over matter kind of resistance to the extreme cold so they can operate without problems. They may be sent to lands boasting below zero temperatures. Such a capability may save his and other people's lives, including his teammates', in an otherwise hopeless situation.

Fun fact: Another concept given of great importance by the US Navy SEALs, and perhaps every military unit, is accurately following orders (i.e. to the letter). Like teamwork and other important concepts, this is continually developed and tested in the trainees. BUD/S is no exception, especially the Hell Week since the trainees' brains are getting hazy due to sleep deprivation. Instructors may test who among the trainees can keep their mental aptitude even with the grueling evolutions they went through.

They may intentionally omit a portion of an order which will reveal who really listened to and, more importantly, understood the orders. As an example, an evolution might involve the trainees lifting a heavy load in a series of orders. Then, for one instance, the instructor will intentionally not mention the load. So, those who listened will not carry the load for that instance. They already get a reward because of the momentary decrease in difficulty. They may also be further rewarded with extra nap-time or a few minutes by the fire.

SCUBA Training Phase

The next phase in the BUD/S is SCUBA (self-contained underwater breathing apparatus) training. The nature of SEAL operations puts them in perpetually "one foot in the water" situations. So, they must be at home in the water. You might have already caught on with that with all the water training such as the surf torture, drown-proofing, and having to carry their rubber boats. An important addition to those is training to operate underwater.

In SCUBA training, SEALs learn to navigate underwater, the efficient use of a SCUBA, combat swimming and diving (both closed and open circuit), long-distance transit dives, and other related skills and techniques. This phase lasts eight weeks.

Land Warfare Phase

Next for the SEAL candidates is the Land Warfare training. Now that they are conditioned for water, they would now need to hone their skills with the element of earth. After all, the SEAL name requires them to be equally efficient in all three elements. This 9-week period trains them to perfect their ground operations.

In the Land Warfare phase, the trainees learn about intelligence gathering and structure infiltration, land navigation, close-quarters combat (CQC), patrolling and long-range reconnaissance, and rappelling. This is also where they are taught to react to special assaults, like sniper attacks. They also train in hand-to-hand combat as well as fighting using bladed weapons (daggers, knives, and the like). They also learn survival techniques in extreme environments (like tropical jungles) and administering field medicine (at least the basics).

An integral part of Land Warfare training is making the trainees experts of small-unit tactics as this is involved in almost all of their missions. They learn how to handle land and underwater explosives, infiltrate enemy territories, perform retrieval operations (so-called "snatch and grab" techniques), and handle prisoners properly.

Parachute Training

After trainees are done with the BUD/S (at this point, only around a quarter of them remains), they will move on to basic parachute training. This lasts for three weeks. They've been trained for water and land. Now, they learn parachuting to conquer the air. SEALs may also be sent to missions where the best way to get to the location is via parachuting. They learn how to land while keeping their team in close proximity to each other. The winds may be treacherous, and if they're not careful, they might be separated from each other or stray too far from the target landing point. Those are not an option during actual operations as they may prove fatal – both to t mission and the men. So, this training, while relatively shorter than the phases in the BUD/S, is equally valuable for any SEAL candidate.

SEAL Qualification Training (SQT)

The parachute training is followed immediately by the SEAL Qualification Training (SQT). The SEAL candidates further train for 15 weeks. This is to ultimately instill basic skills into them – it must come as naturally to them as eating. They also learn new techniques and tactics needed for platoon assignment.

Once a trainee successfully completes the SQT, he will receive his Naval Enlisted Code and the official pin of the SEALs: the Special Warfare Insignia, also known as the SEAL trident or the "Budweiser." This means that he is now an official US Navy SEAL.

The new SEALs will be assigned to either a SEAL team or a SEAL Delivery Vehicle (SDV) team. While they are indeed SEALs, they are not yet deployed on missions. They have some more training to accomplish before they are declared "mission-ready." This consists of different levels of pre-deployment training that lasts 18 months.

The training is divided as follows:

- 6 months of Professional Development (ProDev) – Individual Specialty Training. As you might have concluded by the name, this training is on the individual level. The trainee will then acquire specializations.
- 6 months of Unit Level Training (ULT). This is platoon-level training.
- 6 months of Squadron Integration Training (SIT). This is squadron-level training. Again, teamwork is always central and each SEAL must recognize that they are always a part of a team which is in turn a part of a bigger group which is also a part of an even bigger group.

- SEALs that have a medical rating and wishes to be a medic will need to attend a special 6-month training course: Advanced Medical Training Course. Once completed, he can join a SEAL team as a SEAL medic.

Those who desire to have officer positions will also attend special training: the Junior Officer Training Course. Here, they learn how to plan operations and conduct team briefings.

Starting from the Prep School, it can take more than two and a half years of training before a SEAL is deployed for the first time. But the SEALs that arise are the best of the best – just like how the platoon leaders want.

SEALs receive further training in Special Reconnaissance and Direct Action.

This entails training for:
- Sniper assaults
- Advanced close quarters combat (CQC)
- Tactical ambushes
- Hydrographic Reconnaissance
- Calling in naval gunfire support
- Calling in close air support
- Underwater demolition
- Raids
- Advanced Training

Even after they are ready for deployment, SEALs are constantly training when they are not in missions. They no longer see drills, training, and physical conditioning as something required, but as part of their lifestyle. If a SEAL desires, he can also undergo advanced training. The advanced training develops specializations that come in handy for specific missions. Advanced training includes but is not limited to:

- Foreign Language Training
- Sniper Training
- Jump Master
- SEAL Tactical Communications
- Military Free-fall Parachuting
- Explosive Breacher

US Navy SEAL Structural Organization

SEAL teams are structured under the Naval Special Warfare Command (NSWC). The NSWC is the Navy component of the US Special Operations Command (USSOCOM) which is the overall group encompassing the Special Operations Forces (SOF) of the Navy, Marine Corps, Air Force, and Army. Also referred to as "WARCOM," the NSWC was established back in 1987. The group is formed to take responsibility for the Naval Special Warfare (NSW) forces. It imparts the necessary leadership, vision, resources, doctrinal guidance, and supervision to all NSW forces. It also maintains an international presence of the NSW.

The command of the NSWC is held by a Navy SEAL Rear Admiral (two stars). He administers the mission of the NSWC which is the training, equipment, and deployment of SEAL, SDV, and Special Warfare Combatant-Crew (SWCC) personnel so they can perform overseas maritime special operations. As such, part of the NSWC's responsibility is handling the total budget, doctrine, policies, war plans, training curriculum, and equipment of the NSW. The daily training, operations, deployment, and actual combat operations are designated to the NSWC's respective subordinate commands.

NSWC is also at the head of development of specialized high-performance maritime craft, desert patrol vehicles, submersible vessels, weapons, and gear for the use of the NSW. The maritime craft – low-profile and high-velocity – are operated by SWCC personnel. While relatively new, the SWCC performs a critical role as their specialty lies in covert delivery of the SEALs assigned to perilous areas and their safe and fast extraction upon mission accomplishment.

The subordinate command of the NSW is organized into four Major Commands which are further divided into lower commands. The NSWC acts as the parent command of all these.

The Major Commands are identified as NSW Groups 1, 2, 3, and 4. Under them are eight SEAL teams, two SDV teams, and three Special Boat Teams (SBT). Groups and Teams that are even-numbered are based on the US East Coast while the odd-numbered ones are based on the US West Coast.

The Groups and Teams have their own geographic area assignments (called Area of Responsibility). However, since the forces are composed of small numbers, and they are needed for strategic missions, they may shift focus in critical times. This happens when the US gets involved into major a major war or conflict. For example, during the events of 9/11 and its aftermath, all the NSW commands were ordered to focus to the Middle East. The NSW, as well as other SOF, continues to lead the Global War on Terrorism.

The NSW Groups

A Navy Captain acts as a commander for each Group. During times of peace, a Group mostly acts as a staff unit. They carry out supervision and support the equipment, training, deployment, and the operations of its respective subordinate commands. The Group is also divided into different departments: Operations/Plans, Communications, Intelligence, Personnel, and Research/Development/Testing and Engineering.

Each of the eight SEAL teams has one headquarters element and six platoons. One platoon is composed of 13 enlisted men, one chief petty officer (E-7) or higher-ranking enlisted SEAL, and two officers for a total of 16 SEALs. In general, one platoon is the biggest size for a team assigned for any given mission. Sometimes, platoons may be further divided into four elements or two squads. Each member of a platoon is qualified for parachuting, demolitions, and diving.

Here are the organizational details of the NSW subordinate commands:

Naval Special Warfare Group ONE
Base of Operations: Coronado, CA

Teams

o SEAL Team 1: Western Pacific; Jungle, Desert, and Urban

o SEAL Team 3: Middle East; Desert, and Urban

o SEAL Team 5: Korea; Arctic, Desert, and Urban

o SEAL Team 7: Western Pacific; Jungle, Desert, and Urban

Other Administrative Controls:

o Naval Special Warfare Unit 1 (NSWU-1) – Guam

o Naval Special Warfare Unit 3 (NSWU-3) – Bahrain

Naval Special Warfare Group TWO

Base of Operations: Little Creek, VA

Teams:

o SEAL Team 2: Northern Europe; Desert and Urban

o SEAL Team 4: South & Central America; Desert and Urban

  o SEAL Team 8: Mediterranean/Southern Europe; Desert and Urban

  o SEAL Team 10: Mediterranean/Southern Europe; Desert and Urban

Other Administrative Controls:

  o Naval Special Warfare Unit 2 (NSWU-2) – Stuttgart, Germany

  o Naval Special Warfare Unit 10 (NSWU-10) – Rota, Spain

Naval Special Warfare Group THREE

Base of Operations: Coronado, CA

Teams:

  o SDVT-1: Pacific; Undersea

  o SDVT-2: Atlantic and Mediterranean; Undersea

Others:

  o Worldwide responsibility for NSW undersea mobility

Naval Special Warfare Group FOUR

Base of Operations: Little Creek, VA

Teams:

o SBT-12: Pacific & Middle East; Maritime, Coastal

o SBT-20: Europe, Mediterranean, & Middle East; Maritime, Coastal

o SBT-22: Worldwide; Riverine

12

SEAL Team Six

How is SEAL TEAM SIX different from other SEAL units?

Now you know where SEAL TEAM SIX fit in the big picture.But now you are probably wondering what makes them special and different from other SEAL teams?Lets first look at how regular SEALs are selected.Regular SEALs are selected from regular NAVY units and then go through one of the toughest special forces courses in the world.SEAL TEAM SIX are a step up, even if that is hard to believe, because becoming a SEAL is already a massive achievement.SEAL TEAM SIX only recruit from within the SEAL Teams.The best of the best SEAL candidates gets picked and go through selection.The few that make it through selection go on an eight month SEAL Operators Course.

SEAL TEAM SIX is extremely secretive, and they mostly do missions that nobody will ever hear about.This is how they prefer it.However, sometimes it's difficult to keep their successes quiet.The best example of their success that went public is the killing of Osama Bin Ladin.This story was seen around the world and has even been depicted in movies.

SEAL TEAM SIX members are not the big macho type guys that you see in the movies.They are in exceptional physical condition, but they have a balanced body.They have great flexibility, power and endurance.Their biggest assets are their amazing skill levels and their mental strength.

SEAL TEAM SIX members blend in with civilians and don't normally wear uniforms.They normally have beards, and their hair are longer than the normal military style.These guys are the silent guy next door type.They have a calm presence and easy going attitude.But under the surface they are the ultimate soldiers.

13

Special Air Service

The Special Air Service (SAS) is probably the most talked about Special Forces Unit in the world. The SAS is talked about because it's seen as the father of all other special forces units in existence today. It's the oldest special forces unit in the world and arguably the best special forces unit in the world.

Most of the world was unaware of the SAS until the siege of the Iranian Embassy in London, this event in 1980 made the world take notice of the SAS. Suddenly they moved out of the shadows into the light.

Today the unit is still shrouded in secrecy, but we have a little bit more information about the unit and how they function. The mass media and the publication of many books have given us a peek into the existence of the SAS.

The SAS is the pioneers of modern Special Warfare. They have inspired the creation of many other special forces around the world. The success of the SAS also made governments realize how important the existence of these units are and that no military today can exist without them. The British SAS made other countries realize that they are vulnerable without a SAS type unit in this complex world we live in.

SAS candidates go through some of the toughest mental and physical tests in existence today. If you make it through SAS selection, you find yourself in very select company, not many men get to wear the famous sand colored beret.

Today the SAS are involved in conflicts all around the world, and they continue to lead the way and innovate special operations. When Britain is in a difficult situation, the SAS is called upon to deal with it. They are exceptionally brave men with a famous history. The ethos of the SAS tells you everything you need to know, "Who Dares, Wins!".

History of the SAS

The History of the Special Air Service

The UK's Special Air Service first came to mainstream public attention in the wake of their successful resolution of the Iranian embassy hostage crisis in London in 1980, which took place amidst the glare of TV cameras. Since then, the SAS has emerged as one of the world's pre-eminent special forces units, winning widespread admiration among military organizations for its effectiveness as well as the guile and ruthlessness of its men.

The SAS consists of the 22nd Regiment, which is part of the regular British Army, and the 21st and the 23rd Regiments, which are civilian reservists in the Territorial Army. Its infamous selection process lasts some five months and has a ninety percent failure rate. The six-month course is so grueling and demanding that it is potentially fatal and has even claimed the lives of some aspiring candidates.

The Birth of the SAS

The Special Air Service was originally organized during World War II as a desert raiding force. Founded by Army officer David Stirling on 1 July 1941, it was first called L Detachment, Special Air Service Brigade and was tasked with conducting sabotage missions behind German lines in North Africa. L Detachment consisted of four Army squadrons as well as the Special Boat Section. Soldiers from Free French and Greek squadrons also participated in operations.

The Brigade's first mission was unsuccessfully conducted in Libya and Egypt, resulting in some one-third of the unit killed or captured by German forces. However, their second was a resounding success as the unit raided Axis airfields in Libya, resulting in the destruction of 61 aircraft. The mission was pulled off with the support of the Long Range Desert Group and did not lose a single man. L Detachment continued to run missions in North Africa, although it did perform some missions in Greece, and on September 1942 was renamed the 1st SAS Regiment.

The unit's commander, Stirling, was captured by the Germans in 1943, and spent the remainder of the war as a prisoner. He was replaced by Paddy Mayne, who reorganized L Detachment into two units – the Special Boat Squadron under the command of George Jellicoe and the Special Raiding Squadron under Mayne. The Special Raiding Squadron operated in Italy and Sicily beside the newly-founded 2nd SAS while the Special Boat Squadron conducted missions in the Aegean Islands and the Dodecanese. Eventually, the 1st and 2nd SAS, along with the 3rd and 4th French SAS and the 5th Belgian SAS, was consolidated into the SAS Brigade which ran missions in France behind enemy lines as well as supporting the Allied movement into Germany. Following the end of the war, the SAS was disbanded on 30 October 1946.

The Rebirth of the SAS

The modern SAS was re-formed as a response to the Malayan Emergency (1948-1960), an intensification of the counter-insurgency war between Commonwealth forces and the communist Malayan National Liberation Army. The British had taken control of Malaya following the end of the war and had installed a British Military Administration to govern the country. Malaya was a rich source of tin and rubber as well as minerals such as gold, tungsten, and bauxite, which the British were exporting to earn precious dollars. However, the Malayan Communist Party continued to resist British rule and were threatening to disrupt exports and wreck the local economy.

The murder of three planters from Europe by Communist forces on 16 June 1948 prompted the High Commissioner, Sir Edward Gent, to declare an emergency. In developing a counter-insurgency plan to fight the Communists, it was determined that a deep-penetration unit was needed to enter the jungles where their encampments were located and eliminate them or lead conventional armed forces to their locations.

The 21st SAS Regiment was organized for this purpose and consisted of four brigades as well as the Parachute Brigade Squadron. B Squadron was known as the Malayan Scouts and consisted of British recruits who were originally organized to fight the Korean War. They were joined by A Squadron, which consisted of volunteers recruited locally, many of whom had served in the SAS during the Second World War, C Squadron, who were made up of volunteers from Rhodesia and D Squadron, which consisted of volunteers who had trained at the Airborne Forces Depot in Aldershot.

Small SAS patrols began penetrating the jungles, conducting operations that lasted up to three months while enduring appalling conditions including sparse rations and constant tension. Their efforts successfully prevented Communist forces from effectively using the jungle as their stronghold as SAS soldiers were able to ambush guerillas. They also befriended the aborigines who supplied the rebels with food in order to cut off their supply. The Communists were gradually forced to retreat to the swamps where they were systematically hunted down and captured or killed.

Once the new SAS had proven its value in the Malayan Emergency and the need for a regular SAS army regiment was recognized, the Malayan Scouts were formally organized into the 22nd SAS regiment in 1952. 21st SAS Regiment was also recognized in the same year while the 23rd regiment was established in 1959.

Throughout the remainder of the fifties and the sixties, the SAS was involved in various counter-insurgency operations. In 1958, two squadrons were sent to Oman to fight rebel forces opposing Sultan Said Bin Taimur. From 1963 to 1966, the SAS were involved in the Indonesia-Malaysia confrontation, conducting border patrols to prevent guerilla troops from conducting raids in Brunei, Borneo and Sarawak as well as befriending the local tribesmen in order to gain their assistance in gathering intelligence. The SAS was also stationed in Aden during the Aden Emergency from 1964 to 1967.

In the seventies and eighties, SAS forces were deployed in Northern Ireland, where their participation in operations would eventually become controversial due to allegations that they, along with the Army and the Royal Ulster Constabulary, deliberately killed suspected members of Irish republican paramilitary groups rather than arresting them.

The Iranian Embassy Hostage Crisis

On 30 April 1980, six heavily-armed Arab terrorists invaded the Iranian Embassy in South Kensington, taking twenty-six people in hostage. This sparked a six-day siege during which the SAS created an assault plan as well as an Immediate Assault plan in case the situation deteriorated. SAS planners gathered intelligence as well as studying blueprints in order to get a clear picture of the interior of the embassy.

The shooting of one of the hostages, an Iranian named Abbas Lavasani, pushed the government to authorize the use of force in ending the crisis. The SAS was ordered to begin their assault. The rescue mission was named "Operation Nimrod" and the plan involved multiple assault teams simultaneously entering the first, second and ground floors, assaulting the embassy from all sides.

The assault took just eleven minutes to complete and at the end of it, the SAS had killed five of the terrorists and captured the sixth, although one hostage was killed, and two others were injured. The daylight assault was captured live on television and turned the secretive SAS into a household word while turning their regimental motto, "Who Dares Wins" into a permanent part of British popular culture. The techniques used during the assault were also studied by counter-terrorism units from all over the world and became a standard part of their operational plans.

Throughout the remainder of the eighties, the SAS was involved in some major operations. In 1981, three SAS men were sent to Gambia to assist the government in resolving a coup attempt against President Sir Dawda Jawara launched by Marxist rebels backed by Cuba. The SAS men successfully returned Jawara to office as well as rescuing hostages taken by the rebels that had included members of the president's family.

In 1982, the SAS participated in a large-scale conflict for the first time since the Second World War when they played a major role in retaking the Falklands from Argentine invaders, conducting operations such as the taking of Mount Kent and a raid on an airstrip where eleven enemy aircraft were destroyed.

The SAS also played a role in helping the mujahideen launch missions against Russian forces following the Soviet invasion of Afghanistan in 1979. SAS men lead the rebels in ambush operations against Russian supply convoys as well as instructing them in the use of Stinger missiles provided by the US. However, the SAS were forced to stop providing weapons training in 1982 when Soviet forces discovered two British passports in a rebel training camp. The mujahideen were subsequently trained in secret camps located in remote areas of Scotland.

However, the SAS was embroiled in controversy once again in 1988 when an SAS unit shot and killed a three-man IRA cell in Gibraltar. The operation, code-named Flavius, was intended to stop a reported IRA plot to attack a British parade of military bands by setting off a bomb. However, it turned out that the three IRA members were unarmed, and no remote trigger for an explosive device was found. This led to allegations that the SAS had summarily executed the three men.

Although the European Court of Human Rights found in 1995 that the killings were unlawful, it also ruled that the IRA men had been conducting a terrorist act, making them ineligible to make a claim for damages.

Following Saddam Hussein's invasion of Kuwait in 1991, SAS forces were sent to the Gulf where they are involved in a number of notable operations. When Saddam Hussein deployed long-range Scud missiles and fired them into Israel, SAS A and D squadrons were sent into the Iraqi desert to conduct a search-and-destroy operation against the Scud launchers. The SAS men were sent out in eight heavily-armed land rovers and backed up by Unimog support trucks. They identified installations that could have been associated with the Scuds and marked them for air strikes by US forces. In addition, the SAS columns conducted ambushes along Iraqi supply lines as well as carrying out damage assessment on the battlefield.

However, the SAS was also embroiled in the infamous Bravo Zero Two incident. A patrol with this call sign was captured after being flown into the Iraqi desert on a mission, with four of the men taken captive while three were killed. One of the men, Chris Ryan, was able to escape and walked twenty miles to Syria, from where he was returned to SAS headquarters in Saudi Arabia. The captured men were eventually released by the Iraqis at the end of the Gulf War. The leader of the patrol, Steven Billy Mitchell, would eventually write a book about the incident, titled Bravo Zero Two, and launch a writing career under the pen name, Andy McNab.

The War on Terror

Following the events of September 11, 2001, SAS forces returned to Afghanistan. They were involved in Operation Enduring Freedom, participating in the initial invasion and maintaining a presence in the country. The SAS was also believed to have helped gather the intelligence that allowed the US to locate Osama bin Laden, the alleged mastermind behind the September 11 attacks.

SAS forces also admitted to collaborating with the US Joint Special Operations Command (JSOC) to target insurgents in Afghanistan and Iraq starting in 2003. Working out of a secret high-tech command bunker nicknamed the "Death Star" the SAS reportedly captured or killed thousands of rebels, raiding homes in the hope of finding enemy forces. Occasionally up to four raids nightly were conducted as information gleaned from one raid provided information about another potential target.

In the wake of the withdrawal of US troops from Afghanistan, the SAS has also been allowed to maintain a presence in the country to prevent the Taliban from taking over. Some 100 SAS soldiers will remain in Afghanistan in order to advise and train Afghan forces as well as conducting search-and-destroy missions. However, the SAS will not directly participate in counter-terrorism missions although they are authorized to use lethal force to defend themselves. They will also collaborate closely with Seal Team Six of the Navy and the Delta Force to conduct specific missions such as rescues.

Selection and Training

There are 2 selection opportunities every year, one in the summer, and one in the winter.It takes place in the Brecon Beacons, Sennybrige, Wales.The Brecon Beacons tests the recruits to their limits.The Brecon Beacons is legendary in the Britsh Armed Forces and is known for breaking many hard men.

The instructors are all qualified SAS operators(Operator is a term for members of special forces units like the SAS). Selection is open to all male members of the British Armed Forces, but historically the SAS has been dominated by the 2 Elite British Infantry Units, The Parachute Regiment, and the Royal Marines Commandos.

- **The Parachute Regiment**

The Parachute Regiment provides the majority of SAS recruits. The Parachute Regiment is an Elite Parachute Infantry unit, and they are the British Army's strike force when any crisis breaks out in hotspots around the world. They are highly adaptable and able to deploy at a moment's notice. The Parachute Regiment is one of the best airborne infantry units in the world. The basic training is 30 weeks and to earn the famous maroon beret takes an extremely high level of fitness, courage and determination. The 30 weeks training ends with the famous P Company. P company consists of 8 tests that have to be completed in a week. The Parachute Regiment produces soldiers that are exceptional.

- **The Royal Marines Commandos**

The Royal Marines Commandos is the Royal Navy's Elite Amphibious Infantry Brigade. They form the second biggest group of SAS recruits. The Royal Navy has its own special forces unit the Special Boat Service(SBS), but many Royal Marines choose to join the SAS. The basic training of the Royal Marines is 32 weeks, the longest basic infantry training in the world. The Royal Marines training ends with 4 Commando tests that have to be completed in a week. When recruits pass the Commando tests, they get the famous green Commando beret.

- **Other Units**

The rest of the SAS recruits come from the other combat units in the British Army. The majority of these units are infantry units. However, some come from artillery and armored units.

Selection

About 200 recruits start the phase one of the selection processes. The first thing recruits do at selection is to pass the Personal Fitness Test and the Annual Fitness Test. These are standard British Army fitness tests to get a basic assessment of recruits on arrival.

- **Mountain Phase**

This Mountain phase lasts approximately 3 weeks.After passing these initial tests, they start doing timed cross-country marches.Every day the marches get longer and the terrain more arduous.The loads that the soldiers carry get heavier every day. Instructors at checkpoint hardly say a word to candidates, and they are expected to operate individually.This will be a new experience for many candidates who are used to working in groups of soldiers.Life in special forces demands that operators are self-motivated and be able to operate alone for long periods of time.

The marches culminate in a final march that is called "Endurance." "Endurance" is a 40-mile march that recruits has to complete with a Bergen (backpack) and full equipment.In the march, they must scale and descend Pen Y Fan, the highest Peak in South Wales.They must complete this test in 20 hours.At the end of this test, they must run 4 miles in 30 minutes, and then swim 2 miles in 90 minutes.The Mountain phase is brutal, and many recruits don't make it.Many get injured, and some have even lost their lives.Selection is hard and uncompromising.Only about 15% make it through this phase of selection.

· Jungle Phase

If students survive the mountains, they continue to the 4 week Jungle phase in Malaysia or Belize.Candidates receive training in navigation, patrolling and jungle survival.The extreme conditions of the jungle test the recruit's mental strength.The jungle will also test personal discipline and fieldcraft.In the jungle even a small cut and cause a major infection and lead to death.So soldiers are expected to keep up the high standards that the SAS demands.

· Final Phase

Candidates who make it through jungle training return to SAS headquarters in Hereford, England.At this stage, the group will be very small, approximately 35 of the original 200.In this phase, they receive training in combat survival, foreign weapons, battle plans, and tactics.The final week has two parts; the first is the legendary week-long escape and evasion test. Candidates get placed in patrol groups and carry only a tin can filled with survival equipment.They get dressed in old Second-World-War uniforms.Then they get navigation instructions and get ordered to be at a certain point by first light.In the test, candidates get hunted down by infantry units.

The final test is the second part of the final week.This test is the feared resistance to interrogation (RTI).This test lasts for at least 36 hours and is a nightmare.This test is arguably the hardest and tests the mental strength of every soldier past their known limits.The possibility that a special forces soldier could be caught behind enemy lines is high, so these tests are taken extremely seriously.

It does not matter if you were caught or not in the escape and evasion phase; you have to go through the RTI test. Candidates get treated in extremely bad ways by instructors, and they must resist extreme physical and mental discomfort. Candidates at this stage will extremely sleep deprived, hungry, dehydrated and will be put in physically stressful positions while being questioned.

Candidates get interrogated by male and female interrogators and will get mentally and physically abused. This will test their resistance to extreme interrogation.The 5 human senses of touch, taste, smell, sound and sight get manipulated in a wide variety of ways. Instructors use white sound over 36 hours to create more mental stress for soldiers.The SAS are looking for men who can overcome this mental and physical torture.

Approximately 10-15% of the original 200 will make it through selection.The candidates who make it trough the final phase of training receive the famous sand colored beret of the SAS and gets placed in an operational squadron. The new SAS operators will be probationary members and will receive continuation training. The "real training" starts when the soldiers go to an operational squadron.

This is the SAS selection program in a nutshell. However, large parts of the SAS selection and training is unknown and remains secret.

SAS Squadrons and Units

The 22 SAS Regiment consists of 4 Squadrons.The Squadrons has 4 different specialities although all SAS members can operate in any conditions around the world.SAS troopers that are not officers will lose their previous ranks and will get the rank of trooper.In the special forces community, they are simply called SAS operators.

The four squadrons or troops have the following specializations:

- **Mountain Troop**

This troop specialise in mountain cold weather warfare.They train with equipment like kayaks, skis and snowshoes.They undergo specialised climbing training.They can operate in extreme conditions like the Arctic or the freezing mountains of Afganistan and are extremely adaptable.

- **Air Troop**

The Air Troop are specialists in all forms of parachuting like High-Altitude Low-Opening(HALO) or High Altitude High Opening (HAHO).These operators can be dropped over land or sea and complete their mission.

- **Boat Troop**

The speciality of the boat troop is maritime warfare.They are experts in amphibious skills like scuba diving, kayaking, inflatable boats and rigid raiders(fast light boats).The boat troop has an extremely high amphibious skill set.

They are called in for maritime missions for the following tasks:

- Inserting by small boats

- Maritime Counter-terrorism operations

- Underwater Demolition

- Infiltrate enemy lines using specialised shallow diving equipment

- **Mobility Troop**

This troop focuses on using vehicles to complete their missions.They are highly skilled in desert warfare.All members are trained in motor mechanics and heavy weapons.The origin of this troop dates back to Second-World-War when the SAS would destroy German Airfields with their heavily armed Land Rovers and then retreat to the safety of the desert.These guerilla tactics have been very successful for the SAS.

This troop have the ability to be a thorn in the enemy's side by operating in light, heavily armed vehicles and disrupting the enemy.

Mobility Troop can be very creative with their vehicles.They tailor their vehicles for their needs and turn them into deadly strike force teams.They fit everything they need onto their vehicles that enable them to operate for extended periods of time behind enemy lines.Mobility Troop often creates the impression that a large military unit is in the area with the amount of firepower they create.This creates a large amount of confusion with the enemy.

Troop Composition

The 22 SAS has 4 squadrons with 4 troops in each squadron.Every troop has 15 men that are headed by an officer(Usually a Lieutenant or Captain).In every troop, men are trained in different specialized skills.These skills are demolition, medic, signals and linguist.

Every operator gets trained in all skills, but specialization takes place so men can become extremely specialized in certain areas.This approach creates mastery in certain areas by different individuals.Each troop gets divided into four-man patrols.

- **Special Projects Team**

This unit is the SAS team that deals with anti-hijacking and anti-terrorism.They are trained in hostage rescue, sniper skills and close quarter battle.SAS troops rotate through the Special Projects Team, so the skills are widespread through the SAS regiment.

- **Close Protection**

The SAS is highly trained in VIP protection.The SAS has also been used to train the bodyguards of many British allies.The SAS are regularly called upon to protect British diplomats and politicians around the world.

- **Revolutionary Warfare Wing or E Squadron**

This group is extremely secretive, and not much is known about them.The unit is a group of SAS operators that are attached to the British Intelligence Services(MI6).The nature of their work in not exactly clear, but what is known is that the members are the best of the best and deal with extremely sensitive operations.

Why SAS Operators Are Unique

The SAS remains a world-class unit that still sets the benchmark for special forces around the world.Why are they unique?

- (1)The Idea behind the Regiment

The basic idea of small groups of highly trained men operating independently behind enemy lines is something the SAS pioneered. The extensive experience and knowledge gained in this unique history gives them a distinct advantage. The British Army's extensive expeditionary operation history experience around the world gives them a unique perspective on approaching Special Operations.

- (2)Operating independently with limited resources

The British Army has never been funded as well as the US armed forces have been, and this means they haven't always had access to the best technology and weapons available. This means that the SAS had to adapt their training to focus on the extreme development of every soldier's skill levels to the level of mastery. This gives SAS soldiers the ability to operate independently in the face of extreme adversity and come out on the other side victoriously.

- (3)The title "Special Forces" is not easily given

In the United Kingdom, the title Special Forces is not easily given. The Elite Units, like the Parachute Regiment and Royal Marines, are seen by many foreign governments as Special Forces ,but not in the UK.

The Parachute Regiment is the Elite strike force of the British Infantry. They are a group of highly trained soldiers that go through brutal selection to wear the famous maroon beret. By some, they are seen as a Special Forces unit, but in the UK they are only seen as an elite unit. This means when the SAS select their candidates they come from exceptional groups of soldiers like the Parachute Regiment and the elite Royal Marines Commandos . This leads to exceptionally high standards.

- (4)The Identity of SAS soldiers is kept secret

Unlike some other Units, the SAS operator has to keep a low public profile.The sensitive nature of work means that SAS operators could be targets of foreign enemies.SAS operators will mostly wear unconventional uniforms or civilian clothing when on operations.They grow beards, and their hair will be longer.This gives them the capability to blend into different civilian and military environments.

- (5)The Brutal Selection Process

The SAS selection process is arguably the toughest selection program of any special forces unit in the world.The Selection tests every soldier to his limits.Only the best of the best make it through the selection filter and the ones who make it through goes on to receive the best training for independent operators in the world.

- (6)The Combination of Tradition and Intelligence

The SAS is an organization with a long tradition of doing things in a certain way. However, this tradition is combined with intelligence and efficiency and the mindset of being dynamic and adaptable.The SAS has the capability to come out on top in seemingly impossible situations by being intelligent and adaptable.

14

Conclusion

I hoped you enjoyed this book about the Elite Delta Force .With the war on terror intensifying, the world will continue to depend on the Unit.

If you were thinking of joining the Delta Force, then I hope this book was helpful.

I want to thank you again for downloading my book!

I just want to take this moment to thank the brave men of Delta Force and all other Special Operations Units for their exceptional service, bravery, and sacrifice!

Finally, if you enjoyed this book, please take the time to share your thoughts and post a review on Amazon. It'd be greatly appreciated!

Good Luck!

John Winters

Ó Copyright 2018 by John Winters - All rights reserved.

This document is geared towards providing exact and reliable information in regards to the topic and issue covered. The publication is sold with the idea that the publisher is not required to render accounting, officially permitted, or otherwise, qualified services. If advice is necessary, legal or professional, a practiced individual in the profession

CONCLUSION

should be ordered.

– From a Declaration of Principles which was accepted and approved equally by a Committee of the American Bar Association and a Committee of Publishers and Associations.

In no way is it legal to reproduce, duplicate, or transmit any part of this document in either electronic means or in printed format. Recording of this publication is strictly prohibited and any storage of this document is not allowed unless with written permission from the publisher. All rights reserved.

The information provided herein is stated to be truthful and consistent, in that any liability, in terms of inattention or otherwise, by any usage or abuse of any policies, processes, or directions contained within is the solitary and utter responsibility of the recipient reader. Under no circumstances will any legal responsibility or blame be held against the publisher for any reparation, damages, or monetary loss due to the information herein, either directly or indirectly.

Respective authors own all copyrights not held by the publisher.

The information herein is offered for informational purposes solely, and is universal as so. The presentation of the information is without contract or any type of guarantee assurance.

The trademarks that are used are without any consent, and the publication of the trademark is without permission or backing by the trademark owner. All trademarks and brands within this book are for clarifying purposes only and are the owned by the owners themselves, not affiliated with this document.

Made in United States
Orlando, FL
24 November 2022